P9-AOF-196

Warm Clothes

by

Gail Saunders-Smith

Pebble Books

an imprint of Capstone Press

Pebble Books

Pebble Books are published by Capstone Press
818 North Willow Street, Mankato, Minnesota 56001
http://www.capstone-press.com
Copyright © 1998 by Capstone Press
All Rights Reserved • Printed in the United States of America

Library of Congress Cataloging-in-Publication Data
Saunders-Smith, Gail.
    Warm clothes/by Gail Saunders-Smith.
      p. cm.
    Includes bibliographical references and index.
    Summary: Simple text and photographs present the clothing worn to
keep warm as fall changes to winter.
    ISBN 1-56065-589-5
    1. Children's clothing--Juvenile literature. 2. Cold weather clothing--
Juvenile literature. [1. Cold weather clothing. 2. Clothing and dress.]
I. Title.

TT635.S33 1998
391--dc21
                                        97-29802
            2327   CIP
                                           AC

Editorial Credits
Lois Wallentine, editor; Timothy Halldin and James Franklin,
design; Michelle L. Norstad, photo research

Photo Credits
Cheryl A. Ertlet, 16
International Stock/Caroline Wood, 4
Cheryl R. Richter, 1, 18
Unicorn Stock/Joel Dexter, cover, 8, 14, 20; Chromosohm, Inc., 10;
   Robin Rudd, 12
Willowbrook Photography/Kenneth M. Wiedenbach, 6

Table of Contents

A sweater keeps
my arms warm.

A coat keeps
my body warm.

A scarf keeps
my neck warm.

A hat keeps
my head warm.

A mask keeps
my face warm.

Mittens keep
my hands warm.

Snow pants keep
my legs warm.

Boots keep
my feet warm.

Friends keep
my heart warm.

Words to Know

boot—a heavy shoe that covers the ankle and sometimes part of the leg

coat—a heavier piece of clothing worn over other clothes to help a person keep warm

hat—an item of clothing worn on the head

mask—an item of clothing worn over the face

mitten—an item of clothing worn on the hands

scarf—a long covering for the neck

snow pants—a heavier piece of clothing worn over the legs in winter

sweater—a knitted piece of clothing worn on the upper body

Read More

Bryant-Mole, Karen. *Clothes.* Picture This! Crystal Lake, Ill.: Rigby Interactive Library, 1997.

Fowler, Allan. *How Do You Know It's Winter?* Rookie Read-About Science. Chicago: Children's Press, 1991.

Internet Sites

What Clothes to Wear
http://hammock.ifas.ufl.edu/txt/fairs/3919

Winter Weather Safety Rules
http://weathereye.kgan.com/expert/blizzard/WinterSafe.html

Note to Parents and Teachers

This book illustrates and describes different clothing worn by children in cold weather. The clear photos support the beginning reader in making and maintaining the meaning of the simple text. The noun changes are clearly depicted in the photos. The concrete text changes to an abstraction on the last page. Children may need assistance in using the Table of Contents, Words to Know, Read More, Internet Sites, and Index/Word List sections of the book.

Index/Word List

Word Count: 51
Early-Intervention Level: 4

24